This book is prim̲a̲r̲i̲l̲y̲ ... t is also
suitable for older ... stand, it
adds a ...
between ...

TUDOR REIGAT̲E̲ ̲A̲N̲D̲ ̲T̲U̲D̲O̲R̲ ̲T̲I̲M̲E̲S̲

By Tony Powell

Above: *Warship at the time of King Henry VIII*

Front cover: *1) Coat of Arms of Howard of Effingham. This can be seen on the
fireplace in Reigate Priory.*
2) Earliest known accurate drawing of Reigate Priory.
3) Tudor Rose.

REDHILL CENTRE

FOR

&Local Family History

ISBN 0-9537532-4-7

Printed by
Rayment Printers Limited, 5 Horsham Road, Dorking, Surrey RH4 2JN

**Published by: Redhill Centre for Local & Family History
Redhill Library, Warwick Quadrant
Redhill, Surrey, RH1 1NN
Tel.no. 01737 763332 Fax no. 01737 778020
e-mail: redhill.centre@surreycc.gov.uk
http://www.surreyweb.org.uk/redhill-history-centre**

Queen Elizabeth I. Greatest of the Tudor monarchs. It was during her reign that Charles Howard of Effingham, who lived at Reigate Priory, defeated the Spanish Armada

"The key to a nation's future is in its past. A nation that loses it has no future. For men's deepest desires – the instrument by which a continuing society moulds its destiny – spring from their own inherited experience. We cannot recreate the past but we cannot escape it. It is in our blood and bone. To understand the temperament of a people, a statesman has first to know it's history".

Arthur Bryant

OTHER BOOKS

By the same author

Fire over England
Published 1988

Other books in the series
The History of Redhill Technical School   Tom Slaughter
1926 – 1966

Royalists, Roundheads and Rogues   Brenda Potter
Their connections with Reigate in the 17th century

Redhill, Reigate and District Family History
Guide to Local Records   Arthur Hawkes

Reigate & Redhill in Bygone Days   Tony Powell

CONTENTS

ABOUT THE AUTHOR

Tony Powell was born at Redhill General hospital in 1942 and has since lived in Reigate all his life. From 1953 he was educated at Reigate Grammar School. Between 1953 and 1959 he was very involved in the Reigate Pageants and grew up very interested in history.

Between 1956 and 1971 he was a leading light in the South Park Young Stagers (S.P.Y.S) and founded Reigate Youth Theatre in 1977. During the 70's he was a founder committee member of the local arts council. More recently he has served as Chairman of the Showtime at the Harlequin Theatre up to his resignation earlier this year to allow more time to concentrate on these history books.

About three years ago Tony and his solicitor friend Chris Bell felt the need for a series of local history books and had the idea of applying for a lottery grant to cover the cost of publication. Shortly after it was decided to ask Jackie Johnson, Chairman of the Redhill Centre for Local and Family History to take charge of the project. News that a grant had been approved was received early last year.

AUTHORS INTRODUCTION

This book is about Tudor Reigate and Tudor times, and I have chosen to combine two aspects of Tudor history for three reasons:

1. To give readers a clear idea of what it was like to live in Tudor times. Reigate was much the same as any other market town in those days.

2. To offer schools all they need for a full study of the Tudor period, that fits the appropriate part of the curriculum, as well as a local history. It was suggested when I wrote "Reigate & Redhill in Bygone days" that the book could be used in schools for the literacy hour and I believe the literacy hour should always be used to "kill two birds with one stone" and teach children history as well as to teach them to read.

3. Due to the part played in history by the Howard family, who were very closely associated with Reigate between 1483 and 1675. The Howards were very influential in English history and played an important part in most of the significant events in the Yorkist Age, Tudor England and the early Jacobean years of the Stuart era.

I wish to thank all those who have helped me with this project, especially Chris Bell, my main proof reader and Chris Le Quesne who has typed all my manuscripts and edited the book as well as taking responsibility for the desk top publishing. Arthur Hawkes for scanning the illustrations and Jackie Johnson for generally organising the project and doing a little bit of almost everything.

At the same time I wish to thank the Duke of Norfolk and his estate and offices at Arundel Castle for giving copyright permission for the use of several of the illustrations from the "Norfolk Collection".

Finally I would thank the Heritage Department of the National Lottery fund for providing the funding for this publication as part of the Redhill Centre for Local and Family History's Millennium Project.

Some may recall that twelve years ago I wrote "Fire Over England" to celebrate the four hundredth anniversary of the defeat of the Spanish Armada by Charles Howard of Effingham who was Reigate's most distinguished resident.

Tony Powell
December 2000

AN INTRODUCTION TO TUDOR REIGATE

According to "CAMDENS BRITANNIA"
(Contemporary to these events)

William Camden was born in London in 1551 and educated at Christ's Hospital and also St Paul's School. He studied at Oxford University from 1566 to 1571. After leaving university he embarked on a series of travels around Britain to study local history.

Camden's greatest legacy to local historians was his useful book entitled 'Britannia'. Published in 1586, just two years before the Spanish Armada, it was to prove a valuable starting point in the study of local history for the period in which he wrote.

In his chapter about Surrey he refers to the south of the county and describes *"a continual deep valley, anciently called from the woods Holmesdale, and affording an agreeable prospect diversified by woods, cornfields and meadows. From hence succeed a long ridge of hills and parks well stocked with deer and the rivers with fish, affording plenty of game for hunting and fishing"*.

The town of Reigate, our town, is located in that VALE OF HOLMESDALE. Gordon Copley who edited Camden's Britannia in 1977 adds *"with the North Downs scarp face defining the one side and an irregular sandstone ridge intermittently marking the other, this is still one of the most beautiful of southern English valleys at any time of the year"*.

Camden was our first source for the "rhyming boast" that is today the motto of Reigate and Banstead Borough Council -

"The Vale of Holmesdale
Never Wonne ne never shall"

This means: "never conquered and never shall be". The motto refers to traditions of one or two local defeats of Danish invaders by the Anglo Saxons.

Camden tells us: *"The town of Reigate is large rather than well built, having on the south a well-wooded park in which Charles, Earl of Nottingham, Baron Effingham and High Admiral of England, has a house on the site of a little monastery, founded anciently by the Earls of Warenne and Surrey. On the east side stood a castle, now neglected and decaying with age, built by the same Earls, and commonly called Holmes Castle from the Vale in which it stands. Under it I saw an extraordinary passage with a vaulted roof hewn with great labour out of the soft stone of which the hill is composed".*

Camden became usher of Westminster School in 1575 and Headmaster in 1593. He died in 1623 at the age of 72.

The book was clearly updated through later editions since Charles Howard was not made Earl of Nottingham until 1597. The reference to the "east side" confirms that Reigate Town in Tudor times was clustered around the old market, by present day West Street.

The 'soft stone' was white sand. It is believed that when the caves below Reigate Castle were dug out, the sand was used to make glass.

The description of the Vale of Holmesdale is well supported by a survey of Reigate Priory taken in 1623 and shortly before the death of Reigate's most distinguished resident, Charles Howard of Effingham. The park is described as *"Just over 200 acres .... well stored with tymber trees and replenished with deere havinge allso in the same a faire pond well stored with fishe and a small breede of herons".*

By these descriptions Tudor Reigate sounds an idyllic place, unspoilt by the pollution and planners blight of the 20th century, but for every advantage, there is a disadvantage. There was in those times no electric light or central heating. There was little knowledge of medicine and anybody who lived past 40 years of age was extremely lucky.

Water was drawn from wells or carried from streams and ponds by water-carts. The water was usually contaminated and quite unfit for drinking. The horse was essential when travelling any distance. Most people lived in the countryside and seldom travelled far from their homes.

To recall these ancient names Holmesdale Road and Warren Road are to be found in the north of Reigate beside the railway station. Howard Road and Effingham Road are to the south of the town close to the gates of Reigate Park where Bell Street continues into Cockshot Hill.

Fishing in Tudor England

Today we know much about Tudor England. This is because of the Rennaisance or "Re-birth of Learning" that swept through Europe and reached England at about the same time that the Tudors came to the throne. More people learnt to read and write, and the first printing press had been invented in London by William Caxton in the late fifteenth century. Before that time education and literacy had been virtually a sole preserve of the Catholic Church that had been all powerful in the Middle Ages.

Reigate was a place of considerable importance in Tudor times since it was the home of the influential Howards of Effingham, Lord High Admirals of England, and the story of Tudor Reigate is mainly the story of this famous and important family.

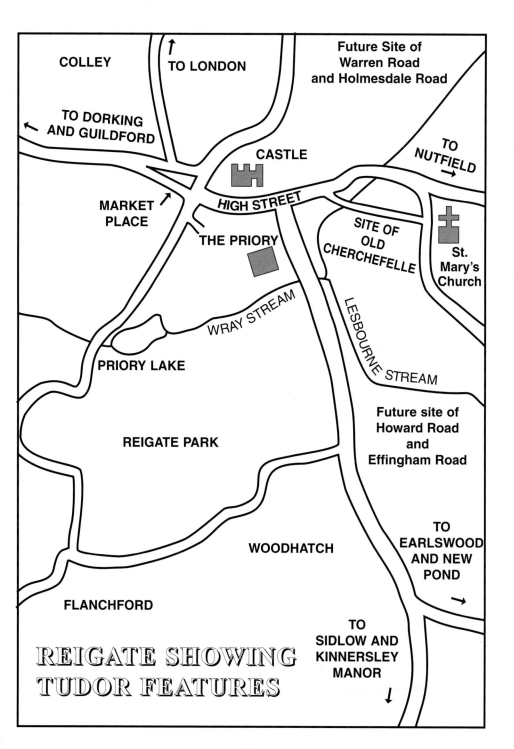

COLLEY

TO LONDON

Future Site of
Warren Road
and Holmesdale Road

TO DORKING
AND GUILDFORD

CASTLE

TO
NUTFIELD

MARKET
PLACE

HIGH STREET

THE PRIORY

SITE OF
OLD
CHERCHEFELLE

St.
Mary's
Church

WRAY STREAM

LESBOURNE STREAM

PRIORY LAKE

REIGATE PARK

Future site of
Howard Road
and
Effingham Road

WOODHATCH

TO
EARLSWOOD
AND NEW
POND

FLANCHFORD

TO
SIDLOW AND
KINNERSLEY
MANOR

REIGATE SHOWING
TUDOR FEATURES

Scenes from the Battle of Bosworth (1485) showing King Richard III and his coat of arms

Arundel Castle in Sussex was the favourite home of the Fitzalan Earls of Arundel. They were also Earls of Surrey and Lords of the Manor of Reigate between the mid fourteenth Century and 1415.

CHAPTER 1

THE END OF THE MIDDLE AGES

The Fitzalans and Mowbrays

Our story really begins in 1415, the year of the great Battle of Agincourt, when King Henry V and a small English Army defeated the French on St Crispin's Day in October of that year.

Sadly Thomas Fitzalan, Earl of Arundel and Surrey, the last of the medieval Lords of the Manor of Reigate, did not live to fight in the battle. He had sailed to France with King Henry V's army but contracted dysentery at the siege of Harfleur and was sent home to his favourite castle at Arundel in Sussex where he died in the same year.

Thomas Fitzalan had been close to the Lancastrian Kings of England, having been disinherited by Richard II and in exile with Henry IV before the latter became King. His death was a sad loss to his King and country.

At the time of his death, Fitzalan was married but had no children. Because of this the Manor of Reigate was divided between his three sisters. The eldest of these was Elizabeth who had been married to Thomas Mowbray, Duke of Norfolk and Earl Marshal of England. The Earl Marshal is a Royal officer who presides over the college of Heralds and organises royal processions and other important ceremonies.

The other sisters were Joan, married to William Beauchamp and Margaret, who was the wife of Sir Rowland Lenthall. Fitzalan's wife Beatrix of Portugal was allowed to peacefully enjoy the Manor and its revenues until her death in 1439.

In the following year, the descendents of Elizabeth, Joan and Margaret agreed to assign Reigate and other Manors to John Mowbray, Third Duke of Norfolk and Earl Marshal. Mowbray appointed a trusted retainer, John Tymperley, as Steward of the District together with full rights to the neighbouring Manors of Gatton and Flanchford. Tymperley served his masters and King Henry VI well and was awarded the right to send two members of parliament to represent his Gatton estate. Tymperley Gardens in Redhill is named after him.

Gatton was an independent manor to the north of Reigate set on the slopes of the North Downs. Flanchford was a small sub-manor to the south west of Reigate including a farm and a water mill where the Wray Stream from Reigate flowed into the River Mole.

In October 1444 Mowbray had a son, also named John, and on 24 March 1451 when his son was just 6 years old the Earldoms of Surrey and Warrenne, which had been extinct since Fitzalan's death in 1415, were revived in his favour. The duke died in 1461 and his son inherited estates of considerable wealth.

The Wars of the Roses

Much happened in the meantime. Henry V had died in 1422 and his son, Henry VI had been crowned King of England at the very young age of six months. Some years later the French, under the leadership of Joan of Arc, began to expel the English from France. By 1450 the war in France was lost and the English nobility were squabbling amongst themselves. Soon afterwards the Wars of the Roses between the Lancastrians and Yorkists began. The wars marked the end of the middle ages in England. The Mowbrays were on the side of York.

By 1461 King Henry VI was deposed by the Yorkist claimant who became King Edward IV.

Marriage of Anne Mowbray and Richard Duke of York. He was later the younger of the princes in the tower.

In 1476, John, Fourth Duke of Norfolk and Earl Marshal suddenly died leaving behind a vast inheritance, including Reigate, to his only child Anne, a daughter who was only four years old.

Edward IV had two sons, Edward Prince of Wales and Richard Duke of York. In order to secure the Mowbray inheritance for the house of York he arranged for his younger son to marry Anne Mowbray in 1478. Three years later in 1481 she died at the tender age of nine leaving her vast inheritance to her husband who was still only a very young boy.

The Rise of the Howards

John Howard, later first Duke of Norfolk. He was killed at the Battle of Bosworth in 1485

There was a rival claimant to the Mowbray inheritance. About 1420 Lady Margaret Mowbray married Sir Robert Howard who was Admiral to King Henry V. Several of his ancestors had been Admirals. In 1422 they had a son named John. Sir Robert died in 1436 and his wife, Margaret, in 1481.

John Howard played an important part in the Wars of the Roses, always fighting on the Yorkist side. He was knighted following Edward IV's first decisive victory at Towton in 1461 and five years later was created Lord Howard. He married Katherine Moleynes, and his son, Thomas, was born in about 1444. Both father and son fought at Barnet in 1471 where Thomas was badly wounded and Lord Howard was at the battle of Tewkesbury a few weeks later. Both battles were Yorkist victories.

John Howard served the House of York as Admiral of High Seas as well as a soldier. In his biography of Richard III, P. M. Kendall describes Lord Howard as:-

"........ plain, solid, tough, a careful householder with a generous heart, a lover of Colchester oysters and of the sea from which they are ripped. The sea was his element. He traded in ships; he fought in ships; ships were his dearest substance."

In 1482 Edward IV invaded Scotland, at that time an independent kingdom. Howard led the English fleet into the Firth of Forth and burned and destroyed the Scottish fleet. It was his greatest victory. In the following year the King was suddenly taken ill and died.

In 1483 the two young princes were lodged in the Tower of London to await Edward's Coronation. The mysterious disappearance and possible murder of King Edward V and his brother, Richard of York, has been the subject of debate by historians for many years. Perhaps the truth will never be known. For a long time after the event it was widely believed that their uncle, Richard of Gloucester was responsible for their murder.

It has also been suggested that Lord John Howard was Richard's accomplice. Richard had the throne of England as a motive and Howard's ambitious eye was on the Mowbray inheritance.

On 6th July 1483 Richard of Gloucester was crowned King Richard III. On the same day Howard was made Duke of Norfolk and Earl Marshal of England. His son Thomas became Earl of Surrey. A few days later John Howard became Lord Admiral of England.

J.M. Robinson in his book 'The Dukes of Norfolk' adds:-

"... So his support for Richard III was handsomely recognised. Or was it perhaps rather more than support for which he was being rewarded".

A half share in the Manor of Reigate was part of that reward.

No sooner had Richard been crowned King than a rebellion broke out led by the Duke of Buckingham who was joined by many of the nobility in the Southern Counties.

It was during the rebellion that Howard visited Reigate where he garrisoned the castle with armed men. He slept the night at the Priory. This was on 13 September 1483.

The princes in the tower

THE YORKIST KINGS (1461 – 1485)

Edward IV

Edward V

Richard III

At about this time, in a letter to John Paston, he wrote:-

"... *the Kentishmen be up [have risen in rebellion] in the Weald, [the central plain of south east England], and say they will come and rob the city [London], which I shall let [prevent] if I may ...*"

Howard raised so many troops and placed them in such strong positions that the rebellion collapsed. Many of the rebels were executed including the Duke of Buckingham.

The Battle of Bosworth (1485)

Two years later there was a more serious rebellion against Richard III. The Lancastrian party, led by the Earl of Oxford were plotting to install their own candidate, Henry Tudor, Earl of Richmond, on the throne. Oxford was an excellent and determined leader.

On 22nd August 1485 the armies met at Bosworth near Leicester. The night before the battle Howard found a note pinned to his tent which read:-

"Jockey of Norfolk, be not too bold, for Dickon thy master is bought and sold".

Undeterred by the strange warning, Howard led the Yorkist vanguard into the battle against the Earl of Oxford and was killed in the fighting. His son the Earl of Surrey was wounded and taken prisoner.

The Battle of Bosworth was decided when Lord Thomas Stanley, who held the other half of the Manor of Reigate, changed sides with the result that the Yorkists were routed and King Richard III was killed.

Lord Stanley offers the crown to Henry Tudor, Earl of Richmond, after the Battle of Bosworth.

Tradition has it that Stanley found Richard's crown in a thorn bush and placed it on the head of Henry Tudor who became King Henry VII and the first of the Tudor Kings of England. The Howards were declared traitors, their lands forfeit to the Crown and the Earl of Surrey was thrown into the Tower of London.

Costume in the time of King Henry VII

CHAPTER 2

LIFE IN TUDOR REIGATE

The Population

Reigate in Tudor times was a very different place from the town we know today. The town of Redhill did not exist, the area being covered with swamps and marshes. The district was not, as nowadays, made up of row upon row of streets with numerous houses. The Manor of Reigate, as it was then known, included the town, which was surrounded on all sides by lush green countryside and rustic farmlands.

The population of the entire manor is unlikely to have been more than 1,000 people perhaps less, and only about two or three hundred would have lived in the town. Most people in those days lived in the countryside. It was a far cry from today's population of more than 60,000. The entire population of England was only about two and a half to three million compared to nearly fifty million today.

About 150 years before the Battle of Bosworth the population of England had been about five or six million, but so many people had died of the "Black Death", of 1348 – 49, that this was reduced to about half when Henry VII, the first Tudor King, came to the throne.

The Town

The town of Reigate, a market town, had grown up in the middle ages, beneath the protective walls of a formidable castle. Reigate Castle was also known as Holmesdale or Holmes Castle after the Vale of Holmesdale in which it stood. It was built to the north of the present High Street. By Tudor times it was already in a state of decay and partly in ruins but it was still in some use.

To the south of the present High Street was a small monastery known as Reigate Priory built by William de Warenne, Earl of Surrey, in about 1235. The priory was situated in spacious grounds and flanked to the south by Reigate Park on the partially wooded line of hills known as the Greensand Ridge. The park was home to deer and rabbits and a popular hunting ground for the local gentry.

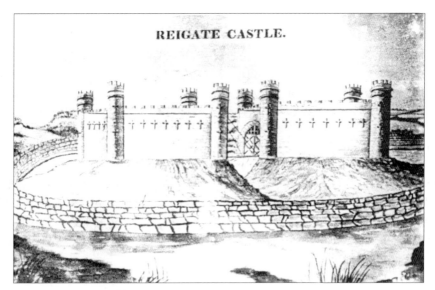

The impression of Reigate Castle from Watson's memoirs of the Earl of Surrey

Tudor architecture today. Houses beside Tower Green in the Tower of London

Sandwiched between the castle and the priory was the present High Street. Running from west to east it was a part of the main highway between Guildford and Canterbury. This part of the town is believed to have consisted mainly of inns and alehouses. At either end of the High Street stood two chapels built on small islands in the middle of the road. A third chapel, dedicated to St Lawrence, stood to the east of present day Bell Street. Part of the chapel wall remains today.

The market place stood at the western end of the town beside the old Red Cross Inn recently re-named the Tap & Spile. Back in the middle ages the Earls of Surrey had been granted the right to hold a market every Tuesday and fairs at several times each year.

The parish church of St Mary stood on the present site about half a mile to the east of the town. The reason for this distance was that the ancient settlement of Reigate, known in its day as Cherchefelle, had once stood beside the Wray Stream but was moved to the west after the building of Reigate Castle for better protection.

Local punishment. The pillory and the stocks

Shops and Market

We know very little about local shops in Tudor times but most goods were sold at the market. There would have been a blacksmith's forge to shoe horses and shape other metal goods like tools, weapons and armour. Perhaps a carpenter to build wooden furniture, an ostler to feed and brush down horses, a wheelwright to replace broken wheels on carts and a barber who was also the local doctor, dentist and surgeon.

On market days, everybody converged on the town from the farms in the surrounding countryside with corn, fruit, vegetables, livestock and dairy products. There would also have been poultry from Dorking, cloth from Guildford and gunpowder from Godstone for local farmers and foresters. Pots, pans, ribbons & trinkets were usually sold by travelling tinkers and pedlars. The baker and pie-man would have baked bread and cooked pies on special premises in the town but sold it either on a market stall or from a tray held to his waist by straps slung over his shoulders. The streets would have been filled with milkmaids, flower sellers and water carriers as all the water needed to be drawn from the stream or local wells.

In Tudor times the Wray Stream flowed openly through Reigate town into Priory Lake and there was a ford where it crossed present day Bell Street.

There were no toilets and it was quite a common sight for residents to throw human waste and the contents of chamber pots from upstairs windows into the streets below. Woe betide anybody passing along the road. There was no street lighting and, in darkness, homes were lit by candlelight or flaming torches in larger halls.

Other features of the town would have included an enclosure for stray livestock and a stocks or pillory for petty criminals and dishonest traders whom the public enthusiastically pelted with rotten eggs, vegetables and filth. There would have been a ducking stool and cucking stools for women who had the cheek to nag their menfolk. Such women were known as scolds.

The Countryside

The wealth of the nation was to be found in the countryside. Descriptions of England at the dawn of the Tudor age have survived. The best description is given by a group of travellers from Venice who visited England about fourteen years after the Battle of Bosworth. They spoke of *"pleasant, undulating hills and beautiful valleys ……….. agreeable woods and extensive meadows or lands in cultivation; and the greatest plenty of water springing everywhere."*

A town market in Tudor times

Tudor architecture today.
The Tudor village at Hever Castle near Edenbridge, Kent.

They mention that *"an enormous number of sheep........common fowls, pea fowls, partridges, and other small birds abound here above measure..."* and for other edible animals they list *"stags, goats, fallow deer, hares, rabbits, pigs and an infinity of oxen...."* Much is made of the wealth of the soil and meat. Also they add *"...it is a truly beautiful thing to behold one or two thousand tame swans upon the river Thames..."*

The Venetians sum up that with the fertility of the soil, the mining of tin and mostly the production of wool *"...the riches of England are greater than those of any country in Europe.......Everyone who makes a tour of the island will soon become aware of this great wealth........for there is no small innkeeper, however poor and humble he may be, who does not serve his table with silver dishes and drinking cups and no one who has not in his house silver plate to the value of at least £100 sterling...."*

Reigate was the chief manor and market town for the Reigate Hundred. A hundred was a medieval system dividing the county for aministrative purposes. Sub-manors included Colley, Santon & Flanchford to the west and Linkfield, Redstone, Frenches and Hooley to the east. All around were independent rural manors. Buckland, Chipstead, Gatton, Merstham, and Nutfield with their medieval churches, thatched cottages and water mills were all a part of the Reigate Hundred which included rural Horley and its several moated manor and farm houses. Hartswood to the south of Reigate was a sub manor of neighbouring Buckland. Kinnersley was a sub-manor of Horley and at Sidlow there was a water mill. The names of Buckland and Hartswood recall deer parks and the hunting that was so much of a pleasure and pastime of the Tudor age.

To the south of Reigate was Woodhatch "the gate to the weald" and to the east of Woodhatch was Earlswood "the wood of the Earl" and, no doubt, another popular spot for hunting the hare, deer and wild boars.

King Henry VIII leading a hunting party

From Bondage to Free Men

Much had changed since Wat Tyler's revolt of the peasants in 1381. The barons and lords of England in the fifteenth century had taken a new and very different approach to dealing with their former serfs and bondmen who, little more than one hundred years before the Battle of Bosworth, had been no more than slaves of the lords of the manor. The new system was known as livery and maintenance.

In his Certificate Library "British History 1965" author C Emmett writes the following about livery and maintenance.

"By the reign of Henry VI, the old feudal relationship based on land had disappeared to be replaced by a system based on a money-and-influence connection called livery and maintenance. It was a system of patronage, lesser men joining with greater for protection and profit. In return for service, usually armed service, a retainer received from his Lord some sort of payment, wore the Lord's badge (livery), and could depend on the Lord to protect him if he fell foul of the law or even if he had private scores to settle (maintenance). Such a system enabled great families to build up private armies."

The existence of such armies made the wars of the roses possible. Both Edward IV and Henry VII introduced new laws to prevent the use of retainers as soldiers.

The Lords dressed their servants in pretty clothes based on liveries of bright and gaudy colours. The shortage of labour resulting from the Black Death was enhanced by the system of livery and maintenance in improving the lot of the common man, abolishing bondage, serfdom and poverty and creating a society of yeomen or free men.

Travel

Few people travelled outside the local area in Tudor times and those who did were usually the lords and more wealthy people. Many of the lords and gentry had lands in various parts of the country and their reason for travel was usually to visit their different homes. Wealthy barons and the monarchy made trips to visit different homes and friends. Each of these visits was known as a 'progress'.

Wagons and coaches were still very primitive and since they had no springs were uncomfortable so that most people preferred to travel on horseback accompanied by friends, relatives and servants, the latter for protection, since the roads were often unsafe on account of beggars and bandits roaming the countryside.

The roads themselves were no more than dirt tracks and unsuitable for wheeled traffic which was usually limited to trade between the towns. Some people did travel, especially if the purpose was trade or military, but on the whole they remained at home and most of their visits were to local markets and fairs.

King Henry VII

Tudor nobility at play in King Henry VII's time

CHAPTER 3

THE RECOVERY OF THE HOWARDS

Henry Tudor

King Henry VII was a Welshman. Before the Battle of Bosworth he was known as Henry Tudor, Earl of Richmond. He had spent most of his life in exile in Brittany and France. At Bosworth he had fought under the banner of the Red Dragon of Wales on a background of white and green. As a result of this, white and green were to become the livery of the early Tudor kings of England.

The Wars of the Roses were so called because of the red rose of Lancaster and the white rose of York. After Bosworth Henry VII married Elizabeth of York who was the eldest daughter of King Edward IV. It was a marriage between Lancaster and York. Their badge was the Tudor Rose, part red and part white and a symbol that the wars were, at last, over. (See cover illustration)

As his personal bodyguard, King Henry VII founded the "Yeoman of the Guard". These were, at first, a company of archers who wore the Tudor livery of White and Green. Much later, perhaps in the reign of Henry VIII, they were merged with the warders of the Tower of London and dressed in the ceremonial red uniforms we know today.

All told Henry VII and Elizabeth had four children. The eldest boy was called Arthur named after the legendary King Arthur of Britain. The second was Henry who would become King Henry VIII.

As soon as Arthur came of age he was married to Catherine of Aragon, daughter of King Ferdinand and Queen Isabella of Spain. These were the King and Queen who had sent Christopher Columbus on his famous voyage of discovery to America in 1492. Sadly Arthur died young and Catherine was re-married to his younger brother Henry. Catherine of Aragon was the first of Henry VIII's six wives.

The eldest daughter was Margaret who married King James IV of Scotland and the youngest girl was Mary who, after a brief and unsuccessful marriage to the ageing King of France was to marry again to Frances Brandon. He was Duke of Suffolk and the son of Henry Tudor's standard bearer Sir William Brandon, who had been killed by Richard III at Bosworth.

Thomas Howard, Earl of Surrey

The Earl of Surrey

After the Battle of Bosworth, Thomas Howard, Earl of Surrey was thrown into the Tower of London as a prisoner, where he was to remain for over three years. He was deprived of his lands and titles including his share in the manor of Reigate.

In 1487, two years after Bosworth, he was offered the chance to escape and take part in a Yorkist rebellion. Thomas Howard chose to remain in prison. The rebellion was defeated at the Battle of Stoke and the Wars of the Roses were finally over.

In 1489 Thomas was offered a Royal pardon and appeared before the King to atone for his support for Richard III. William Camden (see introduction) has attributed to the Earl of Surrey his famous response to Henry's question as to why he was supporting King Richard III at Bosworth. The statement may or may not be true.

"He was my crowned king and if the Parliamentary authority of England set the crown upon a stock, I will fight for that stock: And as I fought for him, I will fight for you...."

A stock means a piece of wood.

Thomas Howard was pardoned and restored to his position of Earl of Surrey, but not, at this time, to his lands or the Dukedom of Norfolk forfeited by his dead father. He was entrusted to be the king's lieutenant in the North of England where he spent much time putting down revolts and protecting the Scottish border.

The Earl of Surrey married twice, to two cousins, Elizabeth and Agnes Tilney. The first marriage to Elizabeth in 1472 resulted in eight sons and three daughters. The future Dukes of Norfolk were descended from Thomas, his eldest son. His other children included Elizabeth who was mother of Queen Anne Boleyn and Edmund, father of Queen Catherine Howard. The second marriage to Agnes in 1497 resulted in a further three sons and four daughters including Lord William Howard who would live at Reigate Priory.

King Henry VII died in 1509 and was succeeded by his son who became King Henry VIII. At the time of his death Henry restored the Earl to his lands.

Thomas Howard making his peace with King Henry VII

"Wide Ranged The Battle on The Plain…"

The Battlefield at Flodden.
The Scots army were originally drawn up on the hill
to the right of the picture

The Battle of Flodden (1513)

In 1512, three years after Henry VIII came to the throne, war broke out between England and France. Scotland agreed to support their "Auld Alliance" with France and King James IV of Scotland declared war on England. King Henry raised an army and sailed to France in June 1513 leaving the Earl of Surrey, now 70 years old, to protect England against the Scots.

King James led an army across the border to invade England on 22nd August and the Earl of Surrey, accompanied by his young son Edmund Howard, marched north. In the borders he was joined by his eldest son Thomas who was Lord Admiral of the fleet and several northern lords including Sir Edward Stanley.

The armies faced each other at Flodden where at first the Scots had the better position on the Cheviot Hills. Thomas outsmarted them by marching his army round the Scottish position after crossing the River Till by Twizel Bridge. Both armies faced their homelands.

The River Till from Twizel Bridge

Twizel Bridge.
Thomas marched his army over the bridge to cut the Scots off from their homeland.

The Battle of Flodden is immortalised in Sir Walter Scott's epic poem "Marmion":-

> *"Wide raged the battle on the plains;*
> *Spears shook and faulchions amain;*
> *Fell England's arrow – flight like rain;*
> *Crests rose, and stooped, and rose again:"*

At first all went well for the Scots as they attacked Edmund Howard's men.

> *"...But Fortune, on the night,*
> *with fickle smile, cheer'd Scotland's fight.*
> *Then fell that spotless banner white,*
> *Edmund Howard's lion fell..."*

Edmund Howard had to fight his way out of difficulty but bravely managed to rejoin his father and brother. The English now attacked the Scots.

> *"The English shafts in vollies hail'd,*
> *In headlong charge their horse assail'd*

*From flank and rear, the
squadrons sweep,
To break the Scottish circle deep,
That fought around their king..."*

It was a charge of the Northern English led by Sir Edward Stanley, on the English left that eventually broke the ranks of the Scots and ensured a decisive English victory. James IV died fighting in the front rank alongside 5,000 of his Lords, knights and men at arms.

Armour at the time of Flodden

Edmund Howard was knighted on the battlefield and Thomas was made Duke of Norfolk, Earl Marshal and Treasurer of England. His son, also Thomas Howard, the Admiral, became Earl of Surrey and the Howard Family were granted 30 additional manors to add to their estates.

Standards captured at the Battle of Flodden

The victory was further commemorated by the grant of a special augmentation to the Howard family coat of arms comprising the Lion Rampant of Scotland pierced by an arrow through the neck. This can be seen on the Howard shield on the fireplace in the Holbein Room in Reigate Priory.

*"That after fight his faith made plain,
He won his rank and lands again.
And charged his old paternal shield
With bearings won on Flodden field...."*

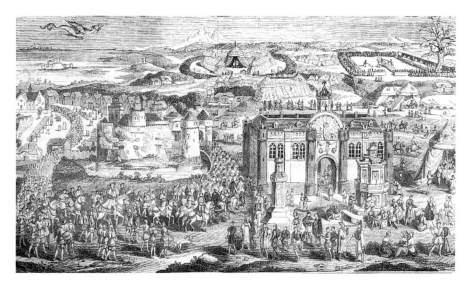

King Henry VIII and the "Field of the Cloth of Gold" (1520)

Queen Anne Boleyn

A few years after Flodden, Henry VIII, who had made peace with the King of France, organised a grand pageant and tournament in Picardy, near Calais, known as the Field of the Cloth of Gold. It was a magnificent occasion conducted with great extravagance and splendour.

Sadly Henry's love life did not go well. Queen Catherine of Aragon had only managed to give the king one child, a daughter named Mary. Henry badly wanted a son and became impatient with Catherine.

The second Howard Duke of Norfolk had died in 1524 at the advanced age of 80 and his eldest son, Thomas of Surrey was the new Duke of Norfolk and Earl Marshal. He was an ambitious man who wanted to see his family more closely associated with royalty.

Anne Boleyn was the younger daughter of Sir Thomas Boleyn and Elizabeth Howard, who was Norfolk's younger sister. The Boleyn's lived at Hever Castle in Kent where Henry and his courtiers often visited to hunt the stags and wild boar amidst the idyllic woods and pastures along the border between Kent and Surrey.

Henry soon fell in love with Anne and decided he wanted his marriage to Queen Catherine to be annulled by the Pope. The Pope took Catherine's side and refused an annullment so King Henry decided to make the Church of England independent of the Pope. These were times of great change with the Renaissance (Re-birth of learning) and

Queen Anne Boleyn

Protestant Reformation against the Catholic Church sweeping through Europe.

As head of the new Church in England, Henry VIII was able to divorce Catherine and in 1533 married Anne Boleyn who was crowned Queen with much pomp and ceremony. Shortly afterwards she gave birth to a daughter who would be the future Queen Elizabeth I.

Hever Castle in Kent. Childhood home of Anne Boleyn

CHAPTER 4

THE END OF REIGATE PRIORY

Reigate Priory

At the time of Henry's marriage to Anne Boleyn, Reigate Priory had existed for about 300 years. It was only a small monastery, or house of religion, compared to the great abbeys that existed in Yorkshire and other parts of England.

The canons of Reigate Priory were of the Augustine order or Black Canons. They were usually bearded and wore black, square cut hats. As well as leading lives of religious devotion the canons spent their time caring for the sick and elderly, teaching the young and looking after the weary travellers who needed lodging and refreshment. There was of course no state-run social security system at this time.

The priory included a church which was built on the south side behind which were the dormitories, chapels, kitchens, a refectory where people could eat meals and an infirmary for the sick. These buildings took the shape of a square, built around an open courtyard, surrounded by cloisters.

The Priory Lake today. The Wray Stream flows in to the right of the picture

The Order of Saint Augustin

A regular Canon of the Order

According to some sources the canons did not eat any meat and lived on a diet of herbs, eggs, fish, bread, cheese, butter, ale or beer. It was the monks who dammed the Wray Stream to create the Priory Lake in order to provide a regular supply of fish and no doubt they kept poultry in the grounds of the priory to provide fresh eggs. Several farms and cottages in the district paid rents to the priory.

The Seal of Reigate Priory

The Dissolution

After his marriage to Anne Boleyn and break from the Catholic Church of Rome, Henry decided to close down all the monasteries in the country and confiscate their considerable wealth for the crown.

Reigate Priory was closed down in 1536. The last prior was John Lymden who became vicar of Reigate Parish Church. Lymden Gardens on the Woodlands estate at the top of Cockshot Hill is named after him.

The new steward of Reigate Priory was Lord Edmund Howard whom we met at the Battle of Flodden. He was responsible for collecting the rents due to the priory and looking after the building. The conversion to a private house may have begun in his time. He died a few years later. The Priory building was more fortunate. After the reformation it became a private home for the Howard family. Many of the former monasteries which were dissolved at this time, were destroyed and became spectacular ruins.

After the Protestant Reformation, people who stood by the old Catholic faith were known as recusants. The Copley family, who were Lords of the manor at neighbouring Gatton, were well known recusants during the reign of Elizabeth I.

An Abbey in ruins after the Dissolution

Bringing in the Yule Log on Christmas Day

Bringing in the Boars Head at a Tudor Feast

CHAPTER 5

FOOD, DRINK AND FEASTING IN TUDOR TIMES

The Dining Table

Food and feasting was very important in Tudor society, likewise etiquette and table manners. However, do not believe the Hollywood image of a Tudor feast - all that business of throwing the chicken bones over the shoulder is pure fiction!

A kitchen in the reign of King Henry VII

In Tudor times there was a clear social structure from the king, at the top of the ladder, to the poorest peasant at the bottom and everybody was expected to know their place. The poor lived on a diet of brown bread and vegetables and seldom ate any meat. White bread was a luxury that only the wealthy could afford.

There was no tea, coffee or fizzy drinks and the water supply was so badly polluted as to be undrinkable, although a still fruit mineral known as cordial had become popular by the late Tudor era. Generally everybody drank beer and ale, or in the case of the rich, wine. The water in these alcoholic beverages was purified by the brewing process. Very often several people drank from the same goblet or beer cup.

Wealthy people employed large numbers of servants whom they treated and spoke to as equals. The appearance of a feast was very important so that servants needed to be dressed in colourful fine clothes to impress the guests. People were expected to sit at the table in order of importance with the King or local lord at the head of the table next to his family and close friends.

The Food

Over half the food on the table seems to have been for decoration and the most popular and important items on a really festive occasion would have included a boar's head, swans and a cockatrice. A cockatrice was made by sewing the front half of a chicken to the rear half of a pig!

Spice and flavouring was in constant use as there were no refrigerators. Other means of preserving the meat had to be used and it was common practice to soak meat in sugar or honey to add to the flavour. This hid the fact that the meat could have gone off! Other preservatives included salt.

A far wider variety of meat was eaten in Tudor times than today. In order to provide a constant supply of fresh meat for the aristocracy, hunting, fishing and shooting of the wildlife were popular sports as well as a means of providing food for the table.

Pigs, cattle, sheep, goat and poultry were reared on the farms but stags and fallow deer for venison, wild boar, and rabbits were hunted down as a sport or shot by forresters, as were geese and swans on the rivers. The Tudor aristocracy also consumed a wide variety of wild birds.

By law, nobody was allowed to eat meat on a Friday. This was originally a religious rule of the Roman Catholic Church, but was kept on after the reformation so as to support the fishing industry. A wide variety of fish and seafood was available. Fish was caught in the sea as well as in fresh water. The most popular fish in England was Salmon.

Tudor feasts are often described as banquets but this is not correct. A banquet was a final course taken after the main meal. Usually the banquet took place in a separate room and consisted of a dessert of biscuits and sweetmeats similar to the crisps and peanuts eaten at a buffet today.

A royal kitchen in Elizabeth I's time

KING HENRY VIII AND HIS SIX WIVES

King Henry VIII

Catherine of Aragon
(DIVORCED)

Anne Boleyn
(BEHEADED)

Jane Seymour
(DIED)

Anne of Cleeves
(DIVORCED)

Catherine Howard
(BEHEADED)

Katherine Parr
(SURVIVED)

CHAPTER 6

THE LIFE AND TIMES OF LORD WILLIAM HOWARD

Lord William Howard (1510 – 1573) was the eldest son of Thomas Howard, Earl of Surrey, by his second wife Agnes Tilney and was the first of the Howards of Effingham to reside at Reigate Priory.

The King's Wives

As we have seen, King Henry VIII's marriage to Anne Boleyn did not go well

Lord William Howard

because she failed to give him a son and male heir. Their only child was the Princess Elizabeth, later Queen Elizabeth I, who, because she was the daughter of Anne Boleyn, was closely related to the Howard family.

Henry soon tired of Anne and fell in love with the young and attractive Jane Seymour. In 1536 Anne was tried for unfaithfulness, found guilty and executed on Tower Green in the Tower of London. Henry quickly married Jane and soon afterwards they had a boy, the future King Edward VI.

Sadly Jane died in childbirth and Henry was soon looking for a fourth wife. Early in 1540 he married Anne of Cleeves but soon found that he did not love her. Prior to their marriage he had only seen a needlessly flattering portrait. The situation quickly led to yet another divorce.

Queen Catherine Howard.
Henry VIII's fifth wife

Thomas Howard, Duke of Norfolk
Uncle of Anne Boleyn &
Catherine Howard

Later that year Henry married for a second time into the Howard Family. His fifth wife was Catherine Howard, daughter of Lord Edmund Howard. Edmund had died and his daughter, Catherine, had been taken under the wing of her uncle the Duke of Norfolk.

Thomas Howard, third Duke of Norfolk and Earl Marshal of England, was the Admiral at the Battle of Flodden. He was a very ambitious man who saw a great chance of Royal favour for himself and his family if King Henry married his niece. At first Henry was extremely fond of Catherine Howard and called her his "Rose Without a Thorn".

Two years later Henry was shocked to discover that Catherine was involved, behind his back, with another man. She was tried for treason and infidelity. In 1542 she was executed in the Tower of London. The affair nearly led to the downfall of the entire Howard family.

Lord William Howard had been a great favourite of King Henry but following Catherine's execution he and his wife were arrested and thrown into the Tower of London charged with concealing the Queen's unfaithfulness. His home at Reigate Priory was, for a short time, confiscated by the Crown but a few months later Henry had a change of heart and the Howard's were released, pardoned, and their lands restored.

A year later Henry married his sixth and last wife. Katherine Parr was a pretty young widow from the Lake

Henry Howard, Earl of Surrey

District who had already been married twice before. She and Henry had a good marriage. By now the King was very ill and Katherine looked after him. He died in 1547. None of his last three wives had given him any children.

Execution axe and block at the Tower of London

A few weeks before his death, Henry had arrested and charged the Duke of Norfolk and his son Henry Howard, Earl of Surrey, with high treason. The Earl of Surrey was executed. His father would have followed him to the block had it not been for the King's own death. As a result of this the crafty old duke was saved but spent several years in prison.

The last years of Henry VIII's reign were marred by further wars with France and Scotland. The French

John Foxe Tutor of Charles Howard at Reigate

were constantly raiding the south coast of England and Henry built a series of coastal forts for defence. It was from Southsea Castle near Portsmouth that Henry watched as his flagship the Mary Rose sank in battle against a French fleet.

Edward VI, Jane Grey and Mary Tudor

Henry was followed to the throne by his only son who became King Edward VI. He was only 9 years old, unwell and died seven years later in 1553 at the age of 16. During his reign the new Protestant Church of England flourished.

Warships and coastal defences at the time of King Henry VIII

Costume at the time of King Edward VI

After the execution of Henry Howard, Earl of Surrey, his children were sent to Reigate Castle for education where they were joined by Charles Howard, son of Lord William Howard. Their tutor was John Foxe who would later become famous for his "Book of Martyrs". Foxe was a forthright Protestant and during his stay in Reigate he stamped out the last remaining local traces of Catholocism. When Mary Tudor came to the throne in 1553 Foxe fled abroad. The Protestant leaders did not want Mary Tudor, the daughter of Catherine of Aragon, as Queen because she was a Roman Catholic. Instead they proclaimed Protestant Lady Jane Grey as Queen. Jane was the granddaughter of Henry VIII's sister, Mary, who had married Charles Brandon, Duke of Suffolk. She was just 16 years of age.

Jane was only Queen for nine days. Most of the people wanted Mary as Queen, and she rode into London at the head of an army and threw Jane into the Tower. Mary insisted that England should return to the Catholic faith and announced that it was her intention to marry the staunchly Catholic King Philip of Spain.

Lord William Howard of Effingham

It was Mary's plans to marry Philip of Spain and return England to the Roman Catholic faith that made her unpopular. Within weeks a rebellion had broken out in Kent led by Sir Thomas Wyatt.

Lord William Howard, at Reigate, was loyal to Queen Mary and suspicious of his neighbour, Sir Thomas Carwarden at Bletchingley. Howard visited Bletchingley Place and discovered

King Edward VI

16 large canons and sufficient weapons and armour to equip 300 men at arms, 100 archers and 50 cavalry. Carwarden was arrested and placed in the hands of the Sheriff of Surrey but later released. It took 17 wagons to remove the weapons and armour from Bletchingley.

Lady Jane Grey

Sir Thomas Wyatt and his rebels marched on London intending to fight their way into the city through one of the gates called Ludgate. William Howard, defending Ludgate with 300 men, closed the gate in Wyatt's face. From the city walls Howard shouted "Avant! Traitor thou shalt not come in here." The rebellion collapsed. Wyatt was captured and executed.

As a result of the rebellion, Lady Jane Grey was executed. Lord William Howard was made Lord Admiral of England and First Baron Howard of Effingham. By this time his services to

Reigate Priory today. It has seen much change since it began as a Medieval Monastry and was later the private home of the Howard family in Tudor times. Today it is a school.

Reigate Priory Lake was created by the canons of Reigate Priory to provide fish. Today it is a beauty spot in Reigate Priory Park.

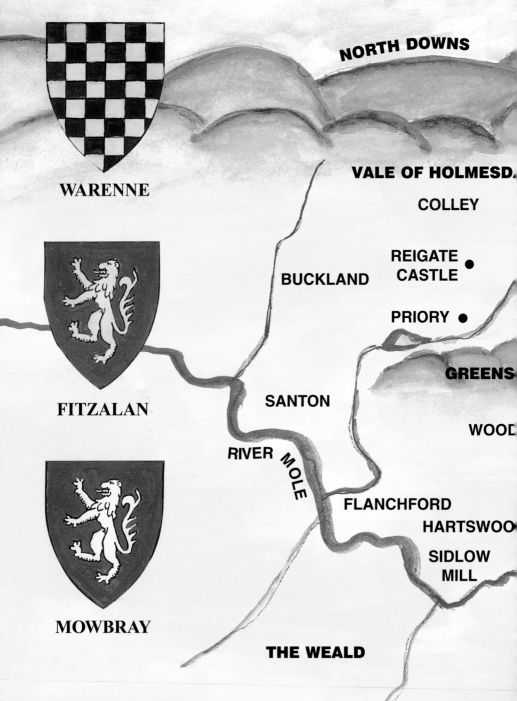

PART OF THE REIGATE HUNDRED IN TUDOR TIMES

WARENNE

FITZALAN

MOWBRAY

NORTH DOWNS

VALE OF HOLMESD.

COLLEY

BUCKLAND

REIGATE CASTLE ●

PRIORY ●

GREENS

SANTON

WOOD

RIVER MOLE

FLANCHFORD

HARTSWOO

SIDLOW MILL

THE WEALD

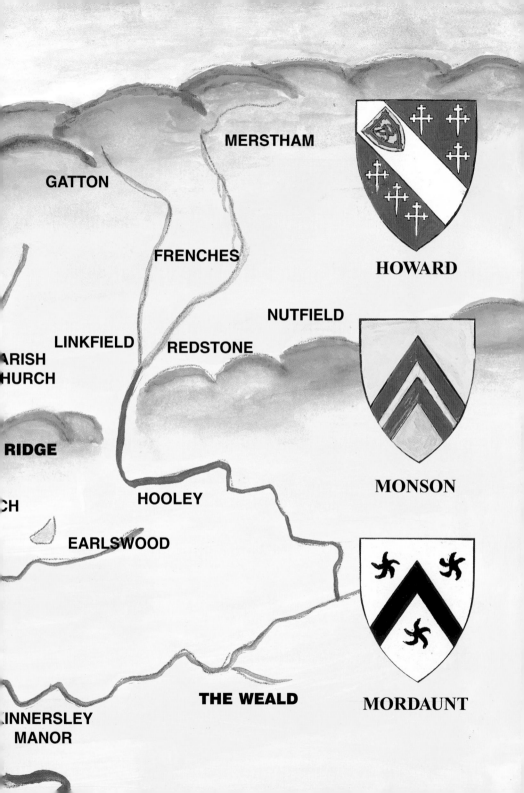

MERSTHAM

GATTON

FRENCHES

HOWARD

NUTFIELD

LINKFIELD

REDSTONE

ARISH
HURCH

MONSON

RIDGE

CH

HOOLEY

EARLSWOOD

MORDAUNT

THE WEALD

INNERSLEY
MANOR

Reigate Castle gateway in the Castle Grounds was built out of stones from the original castle. Charles Howard was educated in the castle by John Foxe.

Reigate Parish Church of St Mary dates back to the Middle Ages. Lord William Howard and Admiral Charles Howard lie buried in the family vault beneath the church.

the Crown had already been considerable. In Henry's time he had made several diplomatic visits to Scotland including the investment of King James V with the Order of the Garter.

During the reign of Edward VI he was governor of Calais, which at that time was treated as part of England. When the King of France offered sarcastically to garrison the town for him Howard replied "The French might come to Calais if they desire but the reception might not be to their taste."

Queen Mary Tudor

Queen Mary ordered her sister, the Princess Elizabeth, to be arrested and thrown into the Tower of London charged with implication in Wyatt's rebellion. The Queen expressly forbade her to have any visitors but Lord William Howard ignored the command and visited and comforted the unfortunate princess. It was later said that Elizabeth owed her life and throne to him... "above all other Englishmen."

Later in Mary's five year reign she prosecuted outspoken protestants and executed or burned more than 300 earning the nickname "Bloody Mary". When war broke out she lost Calais to the French. She died childless in 1558 and Elizabeth came to the throne. It was the dawning of a new age.

Under Elizabeth, William Howard served faithfully as Lord Chamberlain of the Household and later as Lord Privy Seal. He died in 1573 and was buried in a specially built family vault beneath St Mary's Parish Church in Reigate, which is still there today. His prayer book, bound in leather and embossed with the family coat of arms, can still be seen at the Cranston Library in the church.

Tower Green. The site of the headsman's block at the Tower of London where executions used to take place.

Princess Elizabeth is taken as a prisoner to the Tower of London following Wyatt's rebellion

FAMILY TREE – THE HOWARDS

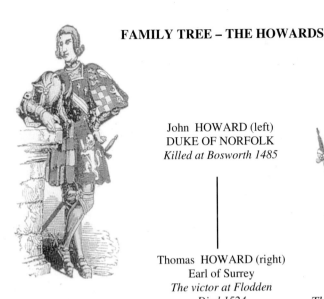

John HOWARD (left)
DUKE OF NORFOLK
Killed at Bosworth 1485

Thomas HOWARD (right)
Earl of Surrey
The victor at Flodden
Died 1524

John, Duke of Norfolk

Thomas, Earl of Surrey

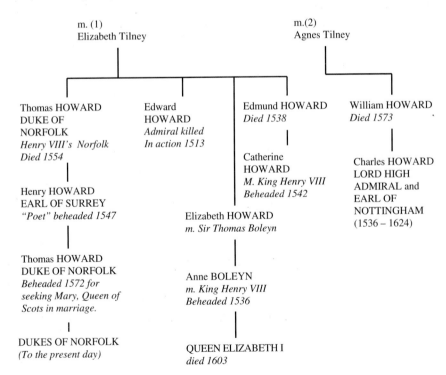

m. (1)
Elizabeth Tilney

m.(2)
Agnes Tilney

Thomas HOWARD
DUKE OF
NORFOLK
Henry VIII's Norfolk
Died 1554

Henry HOWARD
EARL OF SURREY
"Poet" beheaded 1547

Thomas HOWARD
DUKE OF NORFOLK
Beheaded 1572 for
seeking Mary, Queen of
Scots in marriage.

DUKES OF NORFOLK
(To the present day)

Edward
HOWARD
Admiral killed
In action 1513

Edmund HOWARD
Died 1538

Catherine
HOWARD
M. King Henry VIII
Beheaded 1542

Elizabeth HOWARD
m. Sir Thomas Boleyn

Anne BOLEYN
m. King Henry VIII
Beheaded 1536

QUEEN ELIZABETH I
died 1603

William HOWARD
Died 1573

Charles HOWARD
LORD HIGH
ADMIRAL and
EARL OF
NOTTINGHAM
(1536 – 1624)

CHAPTER 7

CHARLES HOWARD AND THE SPANISH ARMADA

Childhood, youth and life at court

Charles Howard, eldest son of Lord William Howard of Effingham, was born in 1536, the year that Reigate Priory was closed down. He was five years old when his father took up residence in the Priory in 1541 and six at the time of his parent's arrest. At the age of eleven, following the execution of his cousin the Earl of Surrey, he began his education at Reigate Castle, alongside the Earl of Surrey's children, with John Foxe as his tutor.

He was cousin to Elizabeth I and when she became Queen in 1558 he was invited to court and soon became a favourite. Most of his time was divided between the court and his family homes including Reigate Priory.

In 1563, at the age of 27 he married Catherine Carey who was the daughter of Henry Carey Lord Hunsdon. Hunsdon was, at that time, Master of the Queen's Hawks and a Knight of the Garter. Catherine was a lady-in-waiting to the Queen and her closest friend.

Charles and Catherine were married in Bletchingley Church. After the death of Sir Thomas Cawarden, Lord William Howard purchased Bletchingley Place.

In 1569 Charles was appointed General of Horse to put down a rebellion in the North of England. A year later he commanded a strong convoy of ships on the English Channel to escort the Spanish Fleet which carried Anne of Austria to Spain for her marriage with Philip II.

King Philip II of Spain

During this mission Lord Charles Howard *"environed the Spanish fleet in most strange and warlike sort, and forced them to stoop gallant and to vail their bonnets to the Queen of England."*

When his father died in 1573, Charles Howard became Baron Howard of Effingham. In 1574 he was made a Knight of the Garter and, about the same time, Lord Chamberlain of the Household.

As Chamberlain he was responsible for the Royal Wardrobe, jewel house and the Royal kitchens, bakery, spicery and banqueting hall as well as lodgings in the Royal Palaces. Then there were the Royal Chaplains, chapel vestry, surgeons, apothocaries, painters, astronomers, mole takers and Master of Hounds, Royal Parks and deer herds, the Queens Ordinance, the Royal Mint and amongst all sorts of other duties the reception of foreign ambassadors at court.

The Enterprise of England

In the meantime dramatic events were taking place in the world at large. Since Christopher Columbus had discovered America, "The New World", in 1492, Spain had become the wealthiest and most powerful nation in Europe. They had established a vast empire in the "New World" and richly loaded galleons brought home cargoes of gold, silver, spices and other goods of considerable value.

With Europe divided between Protestants and Catholics, Spain had become the champion of the Roman Catholic Faith. The Spanish inquisition had a fearsome reputation for burning and torturing any

Protestants who fell into their hands. As Catholics were known to Protestants as "Recusants", so Protestants were described by Catholics as "Heretics".

In Scotland King James V had been succeeded by his daughter, Mary Queen of Scots who was a devout Catholic. Most of the Scots became Protestant and rebelled against Mary. She was defeated in battle and forced to flee to England in 1568. When she arrived she threw herself on the mercy of her cousin Queen Elizabeth.

Mary Queen of Scots.
Executed 1587

In England, Elizabeth held Mary captive for nearly twenty years. Mary, in turn, became the centre of several Catholic plots against Elizabeth. The Pope in Rome decided that Elizabeth should be excommunicated. That is excluded from all services and prayers of the church. Excommunication was a serious matter in these times. The Pope then appealed to King Philip of Spain to take steps to return England to the Roman Catholic Faith.

Sir Francis Drake

The result was undeclared war. Elizabeth turned a blind eye when enterprising seamen such as Francis Drake and John Hawkins set sail to capture Spanish galleons on the high seas and raid Spanish ports in the "New World". On one occasion Francis Drake, in his ship The Pelican, later named the Golden Hinde, sailed round the world and returned to England laden with riches. To the Spanish, Drake "El Draco" was not only a heretic but a

Charles Howard of Effingham

pirate. In an act of outright provocation Elizabeth knighted Sir Francis Drake for his enterprise and patriotism.

In 1587, following another Catholic plot, Elizabeth ordered Mary Queen of Scots to be executed. It was the final straw. Philip of Spain declared war on England and put together a vast armada of ships to convey his troops in an outright invasion. It was known as the "Enterprise of England".

Charles Howard becomes Lord Admiral

In May 1585, Charles Howard was appointed as Lord Admiral of England. He was replaced as Lord Chamberlain by his father-in-law, Lord Hunsdon. Queen Elizabeth described him as: *"skillful in nautical affairs, wary and prudent and that by the sweetness of his behaviour and by his bravery and conduct he was of great authority and esteem among the seamen."*

In 1587 he raised his flag above the Ark Royal and set out to inspect the English Fleet:

"I protest before God, and as my soul shall answer for it, that I think were never in any place in the world worthier ships than these are, if the king of Spain's forces be not hundreds, we will make good sport of them. And I pray you tell her majesty from me that her money was well given for the Ark Royal, for I think her the odd (one) ship in the world for all conditions, and truly I think there can be no great ship to make me change and go out of her."

Howard of Effingham to Lord Burleigh

In the summer of the following year the Spanish Armada set sail. Their instructions were to sail up the English Channel to the Netherlands and there collect an army under the Duke of Parma and carry them to invade England. Late in July they were sighted off the Lizard Peninsular in Cornwall. Howard and a large part of his fleet were at Plymouth. They set sail on the following day, Howard in the "Ark Royal" leading out! *"the gallantest company of captains, soldiers, and mariners that I have ever seen in England."*

The Defeat of the Spanish Armada

Howard and the English sea captains did not know the Spanish plan to set sail to the low countries and embark Parma's army. For all they knew the Spanish fleet could land at any time or place. The Armada sailed up the channel in a crescent formation.

The English ships kept at a distance exchanging cannon shots with the Spaniards. Since the English ships were smaller and faster they sustained very little damage whereas a number of Spaniards were crippled, captured by the English, and taken into the port of Torquay as prizes of war.

The "Ark Royal" flagship of Admiral Charles Howard of Effingham

Charles Howard wrote *"Their force is wonderful great and strong and yet we pluck their feathers little by little."*

For nearly a week the battle continued up the channel with the fleets fighting in the daytime and sailing on at night.

"The fight was very nobly continued from morning 'til evening, the Lord Admiral being always in the hottest of the encounter.." wrote one English sea captain. Howard added *"we durst not put in among them, their fleet being so strong."*

A week of battles off Plymouth, Portland Bill and the Isle of Wight was watched by crowds of English on the shore. None really knew what was happening since all they could see were the ships and puffs of smoke from their cannons. When Howard sent word to the shore that he was running short of supplies and ammunition hundreds of small boats put out to sea to replenish the English Fleet.

Eventually the Spanish anchored in Calais harbour and, following a council of war, Howard and his captains decided to disburse the enemy with fireships. The terrified Spaniards broke their moorings and fled in disorder to Gravelines where they were attacked and routed by the English fleet.

The Spanish Armada now set sail for home via Scotland and Ireland but were soon subjected to heavy winds, storms and gales with the result that many of the galleons were sunk or washed ashore on the hostile coast. Howard's victory was decisive and England was saved from invasion.

CHAPTER 8

QUEEN ELIZABETH AND MERRIE ENGLAND

Tilbury August 1588

While Charles Howard was defeating the Spanish Armada in the English Channel, and chasing the routed enemy fleet into the North Sea, Queen Elizabeth had raised an army for the defence of London. The troops were assembled at Tilbury for a grand ceremonial review. Queen Elizabeth addressed them with a famous speech which has been preserved. It began with the words *"My loving people...."* And continued *"Let tyrants fear."*

"I am come amongst you, as you see, resolved, in the midst and heat of battle, to live or die amongst you all, to lay down for my God, and for my kingdom, and for my people, my honour and my blood, even in the dust.

I know I have the body of a weak and feeble woman, but I have the heart and stomach of a king, and of a king of England too, and think foul scorn that Parma or Spain or any Prince of Europe should invade the borders of my realm; to which,......... I myself will take up arms, I myself will be your general, judge and rewarder..... We shall shortly have a famous victory over those enemies of my God, of my Kingdom and of my people."

This was perhaps Elizabeth's most shining moment. The victory over the Armada was followed by an age that was both glamorous and prosperous.

It was a time of change and novelty. Sailors returned from voyages to the "New World" with stories of strange lands and strange people having come face to face with the native Americans of the West Indies and American mainland. Exotic fruits like pineapples and vegetables such as the potato were brought home to England as well as tobacco.

The colony of Virginia was named after Queen Elizabeth I "The Virgin Queen" and another, Maryland, after her sister Queen Mary, became the home of recusant Catholics who did not wish to live in Protestant England.

Queen Elizabeth and her court

Festivals and Holidays

The idea of public holidays when nobody worked and everybody enjoyed themselves with festivities and merrymaking with song, dance and special food and drinking had grown out of the old traditions of the Catholic Church.

Holidays were Saint's days or Holy days. The Church had many saints so there were no shortage of holidays and festivals in Tudor times. The most important holiday was Christmas and the most popular was Mayday.

The Christmas festival began on Christmas day and lasted for twelve days of feasting and celebration, ending in grand style on Twelfth Night when the festivities reached their climax. St Valentine was the patron saint of lovers and St Crispin was the patron saint of shoemakers. Midsummers night was the shortest night of the year following the longest day and a great time for celebration.

Merrymaking in Tudor England

William Shakespeare, who lived in Elizabeth I's reign, wrote plays called "Twelfth Night" and "A Midsummers Night's Dream" and this demonstrates the importance of these occasions to the people of Tudor England. In his play "King Henry V" much is made of the fact that the Battle of Agincourt was fought on St Crispin's Day.

May Day was the most popular of the holidays and festivals in Tudor times. It marked the end of winter and the start of summer. It was a time when leaves were appearing on the trees, flowers were blooming and spring lambs were prancing in the meadows to the tune of birds singing.

Young girls vied with each other in arranging their hair with garlands of flowers. The prettiest girl was crowned Queen of the May and everybody danced around maypoles to the sounds of bands of musicians followed by morris dancing, mumming (acting out short plays) and the inevitable feasting and drinking of mead and cider The feasting usually consisted of roasting a whole hog or cow on a spit in the open air.

A typical English maypole

The Elizabethan Theatre

The late Elizabethan age was famous for the rise of the theatre. Early theatres were built in an oval shape with only the wealthy gentry seated under cover from the rain. Ordinary people known as "groundlings" had to stand in the open air. When a play was to be performed it was customary to raise a flag and sound a trumpet from a tower built over the stage. There is a modern reconstruction of the Globe Theatre on London's South Bank.

For a company of players to perform they needed, by law, to obtain the patronage of an influential Lord. Admiral Charles Howard of Effingham was such a patron. His company was known as "The Admirals Men" and was run by Philip Henslow whose account book has survived to this day. The book contains valuable information about the early theatre.

The best actor in "The Admirals Men" was Edward Alleyn, Henslow's son-in-law who later founded Dulwich College. The company performed plays by such playwrights as Thomas Kyd, Christopher Marlowe and Thomas Dekker.

Their rivals were the Lord Chamberlain's Men whose patron was Lord Hunsdon. They were run by James Burbage and their best actor was his son Richard Burbage. Their great claim to fame was that William Shakespeare was a member of the company. He was unquestionably the greatest playwright ever and he wrote nearly forty plays.

The Globe Theatre

Shakespeare's most famous play was Hamlet. Many of the

phrases from this play such as "there is method in his madness" and "hoisted on his own petard" have become an everyday part of the English language.   Other plays were political such as Richard III which glorifies the part played by the Tudors in winning and ending the Wars of the Roses.   King Richard was portrayed as an evil villain. His death at the Battle of Bosworth . *"A horse, a horse, my kingdom for a horse"* is a classic and favourite Shakespearean scene. Shakespeare was, however, known to re-write history on occasions!

Other popular entertainment in Tudor times consisted of sport involving much cruelty to animals.   These included cock fighting and baiting bears with hungry dogs.   Today such sports are illegal.

The End of the Tudor Era

Meantime the war with Spain continued.   In 1596 Admiral Charles Howard of Effingham and Queen Elizabeth's favourite, Robert Devereux, Earl of Essex, were given joint command of an expedition to Cadiz harbour.   Their purpose was to destroy the Spanish fleet and teach the King of Spain a lesson that would end any further threat of invasion.

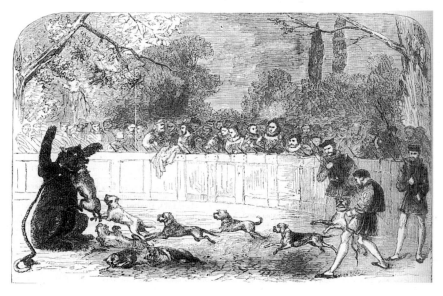

Baiting bears with dogs in Tudor times

Robert Deveraux, Earl of Essex

Howard commanded the fleet at sea and Essex the troops on land. The battle was a complete victory for the English. The Spanish fleet was destroyed in the harbour and the city of Cadiz was stormed and sacked by the triumphant English soldiers and sailors.

Queen Elizabeth wrote to Howard and Essex *"You have made me famous, dreadful and renowned, not more for your victory than for your courage.."*. On 22nd October 1597 Charles Howard was created Earl of Nottingham and two years later in 1599 was appointed Lord Lieutenant General of all England. This meant he had command of the army as well as the navy. No other Englishman has ever held such a high military position before or since.

Charles Howard had become the most important person in England save only the Queen. All told he owned seven houses including Reigate Priory. The others were Arundel House in the Strand, London, Skynners Place near Greenwich, Bletchingley Place, Effingham Manor, Haling House in Croydon and Chelsea Manor House.

In February 1601 the Earl of Essex foolishly embarked on a rebellion that was to cost him his life. He had been very jealous of Charles Howard since the latter had been made Earl of Nottingham. Elizabeth found it very difficult to sign Essex's death warrant but Howard, who stood high in the Queen's favour, offered her comfort.

Two years later in February 1603 Howard's wife Catherine died, to be followed a few days later by Queen Elizabeth herself. Elizabeth, "the Virgin Queen" had never married and had no children or immediate heir to succeed her to the throne.

Elizabeth called Charles Howard to her deathbed and named James VI of Scotland as her successor. James was the son of Mary Queen of Scots and next in line to succeed the English throne. This was the result of Henry VII's decision to marry his daughter Margaret to King James IV a century earlier in 1502.

Arundel House in the Strand

CHAPTER 9

AFTERMATH

The Last Years of Charles Howard

The above miniature of Charles Howard of Effingham can be found on his monument in Reigate Parish Church of St Mary

After the death of his first wife, Charles Howard had married a second time in 1604 to the young Margaret Stuart, daughter of the Scottish Earl of Murray. It was his two separate and very different marriages that led to the problems and complications that followed his death.

Charles Howard died in 1624 at Haling House, Croydon. He had reached, for those days, the ripe old age of 87 and his last letters show that he remained sound in mind and body to the end. His body was taken to Reigate and he was buried at midnight on 23rd December in the family vault at Reigate Parish Church where, according to his will: *"...my late lorde and father lyeth buried in such honourable state...".*

Since the death of Queen Elizabeth I, Charles Howard had led the peace mission to Spain where he and his retinue were well treated. He had also sat on the commission to try the conspirators in the Gunpowder Plot.

The Gunpowder Plot, 1605, was an attempt by a group of Catholics to blow up the Houses of Parliament while the new Protestant King James I was inside. Several barrels of gunpowder were placed in the cellars and a man called Guy Fawkes agreed to light the fuse. The plot was discovered and the conspirators arrested. Every year the plot is recalled by Guy Fawkes night on the 5th November.

"Remember, remember the 5th of November
Gunpowder, treason and plot.
We see no reason why gunpowder treason
Should ever be forgot."

The Ownership of Reigate Priory

No sooner had Charles Howard died than his young widow married again. Her husband was John Lord Monson & Viscount Castlemaine who lived at nearby Kinnersley Manor and had once been her page. Margaret and Lord Monson were married at Reigate Parish Church in 1625. The wedding was considered to be an important local event.

As a result of his marriage, Lord Monson became Lord of the Manor of Reigate. He soon made himself very unpopular with the local people by enclosing Reigate Park and cutting down the trees on the local commons, including Earlswood, and turning them into rabbit warrens.

St Mary's Parish Church, Reigate

When his wife died in 1639 the next heir to Reigate Priory was Elizabeth, Countess of Peterborough, who was Charles Howard's granddaughter from his first marriage to Catherine Carey. When Elizabeth claimed Reigate Priory, but Monson, who was in possession, resisted her claim and went so far as to call out the local militia and place a cannon at the entrance to the grounds. In order to gain possession of the Priory, Elizabeth was forced to seek help from the courts and eventually succeeded.

Elizabeth had married John, Lord Mordaunt of Turvey at Bletchingley Place in 1621. The fortunes of the Mordaunt family had been founded at the Battle of Stoke in 1487 when an earlier John Mordaunt was rewarded for his services to Henry VII with the position of Speaker of the House of Commons. Little is known of the family in Tudor times because they were recusants.

In 1605 the father of John, Lord Mordaunt was, as a Catholic, suspected of involvement in the Gunpowder Plot and thrown into the Tower of London for a year. King James was determined that Mordaunt's son should be brought up in the Protestant faith and he was made a Ward of Archbishop Abbot of Canterbury. He was educated at Oxford and knighted in 1616. John & Elizabeth had two sons, Henry and John.

The fireplace in Reigate Priory showing the arms of Howard.
The oaken chimney piece was added in the 1650's.

The English Civil War

In 1642 the Civil War broke out between the Cavaliers (Royalists) and Roundheads (Parliament). The Peterboroughs joined the Roundheads. Lord Monson also joined the Roundheads and was a committee man for Surrey. Lord Peterborough died of illness in the first year of the war and Henry, who became Earl of Peterborough, changed sides and joined the Royalists. He was wounded in the thigh at the first battle of Newbury. At that time his brother John was still quite young but his sympathies, too, lay with the Royalists.

After the first Civil War ended in 1646 in victory for the Roundheads many troops were quartered with the people in Surrey and there were several unpleasant incidents between the people and the soldiers. In Reigate, a serious riot broke out in February 1648 and, as a result, two civilians were killed.

The people of Surrey held a public meeting in Dorking and decided to petition parliament for the withdrawal of troops and restoration of the King. In May, the men of Surrey marched on London with oak leaves decorating their hats and flags flying. The result was a riot outside the Palace of Westminster and several of the petitioners as well as some soldiers were killed.

A month later the Second Civil War broke out and a party of Royalists led by the Earl of Holland marched into Surrey expecting the petitioners would flock to their standards. Holland was joined by the Duke of Buckingham, his brother Francis Villiers, Henry and John Mordaunt.

The Royalists took Reigate Castle and set up pickets on Redhill Common but these were driven in by the Roundheads after a short sharp skirmish and the Royalists were forced to retreat to Surbiton where they were defeated in battle and Francis Villiers was killed. Henry Mordaunt was, for a second time, driven into exile abroad.

The Commonwealth 1649 - 1660

The result of the second Civil War was total victory for Parliament and early in the following year, 1649, King Charles I was executed. His son, soon to be King Charles II, had already been driven into exile.

Parliament imposed a Puritan republic on England based on the beliefs of a non-conformist Christianity. Oliver Cromwell became Lord Protector. People were expected to dress in sombre clothes and lead sombre lives. All holidays, and festivals including Christmas were curtailed and became illegal. Dancing and singing (apart from Psalms) were not permitted. The theatres were closed down.

Very soon the people of England became fed up and wanted Charles II back on the throne and dedicated bands of Royalists worked secretly to organise a Restoration. John Mordaunt was particularly active in these activities. In 1658 he was arrested and put on trial for High Treason. He was acquitted by a single vote. The main reason being that Oliver

Cromwell was dying and many of his judges feared the consequences of a Royalist Restoration. Cromwell died soon afterwards. Charles II made Mordaunt Viscount Avalon and Baron Mordaunt of Reigate.

In 1659 John Mordaunt tried to organise a Royalist rebellion or rising at Redhill Common but the authorities were alerted and the Cavaliers were forced to make a run for it. At Shellwood near Leigh they were defeated and dispersed. Mordaunt fled back to France where he was active in the Restoration of King Charles II in 1660.

Restoration and Glorious Revolution

After the Restoration, Lord Monson (who had been loyal to Parliament), was put on trial as a Regicide. A Regicide was a party to the execution of Charles I. He was thrown into the Tower of London where he died in 1671. He was stripped of the Manor of Reigate which was awarded to the King's younger brother, James, Duke of York. John Mordaunt died in 1675 and his brother Henry put Reigate Priory up for sale. In 1681 it was purchased by John Parsons.

King Charles II died in 1685 and James, Duke of York, became King James II. He was a Catholic and tried to return England to the Roman Catholic faith, but only served to make himself very unpopular. Henry Mordaunt supported James and joined the Catholic faith but his Protestant nephew, Charles Mordaunt, son of John and later Earl of Peterborough sailed for Holland. He was the first English statesman to invite William of Orange to invade England and become King.

In 1688 William landed with his army at Brixham in Devon. Most of James' army defected to William and James himself fled into exile. The event was known as "The Glorious Revolution". Henry Mordaunt was arrested and had to spend some time in prison. Later, when Henry died, Charles Mordaunt became Earl of Peterborough and played a significant part in the wars of Queen Anne and the Duke of Marlborough against France.

When James II fled he was stripped of all his lands and titles including the Manor of Reigate. In 1697 William II granted the Manor of Reigate to his Chancellor Lord Somers whose family remained Lords of the Manor for more than 200 years.

Chancellor Lord Somers

The story of Reigate and Redhill continues in "Reigate & Redhill in Bygone Days". Copies now available.

For full details of the period covered in this chapter see: Royalists, Roundheads and Rogues – Brenda Potter

PLACES OF INTEREST TO VISIT

Arundel Castle

Set on a vast estate in Sussex, Arundel Castle is the property of the present day Duke of Norfolk and Earl Marshal of England. The castle is open to the public six days a week and closed on Saturdays.

The castle is the ancestral home of the Fitzalans and the Howards, having been passed to the Howards in 1580. It is also the home of a massive wealth of Howard history and filled with the paintings, family heraldry and books. It is an excellent place for historical research on the Howards and Fitzalans.

The Howard flag flies over the keep which is the oldest part of the castle.

Hever Castle

Located about three miles from the town of Edenbridge, near the border between Kent and Surrey, Hever Castle is set in the midst of attractive grounds and gardens. It is open to the public.

Hever Castle was the family home of Anne Boleyn and it was here that she was courted by King Henry VIII. She was the granddaughter of Thomas Howard, Earl of Surrey and cousin of Charles Howard of Effingham. It was due to this that Charles Howard was a close kinsman of Queen Elizabeth I.

More recently, the castle came into the possession of the Astor family who renovated the contents and grounds as a tourist attraction.

The Tower of London

As one of Britain's most popular tourist attractions, most of the tower remains much the same today as it was in Tudor times. Then it was a palace and a prison as well as containing a managerie and the Royal Mint. Today it is famous as the home of the Crown Jewels.

At the tower it is possible to see the "Traitors Gate" where prisoners were brought into the fortress after being transported down river and the "Bloody Tower" where many of them were housed. On Tower Green it is possible to see the site of the "headsman's block" where many of the characters mentioned in this book were executed.

Hampton Court Palace

A short distance from Kingston on Thames, Hampton Court Palace was acquired by King Henry VIII at the time of his marriage to Anne Boleyn. Set in spacious grounds, the palace includes an indoor Tudor tennis court and well preserved kitchens of the Tudor era.

In March/April each year the grounds include fields of magnificent daffodils and narcissus, and between Easter and September the Palace and grounds can be reached from Kingston on Thames by pleasure craft.

Southsea Castle

Not far from Portsmouth Harbour and open to the public is Southsea Castle. It is an excellent example of the coastal defences built by King Henry VIII.

The castle offers magnificent views across The Solent to the Isle of Wight. It was from Southsea Castle that King Henry VIII watched the sinking of the "Mary Rose" in 1546.

The "Mary Rose" was excavated and raised in the early 80's and it's remaining timbers can be seen at Portsmouth Harbour together with other historic ships.

FURTHER READING

Reigate, it's story through the ages	W Hooper
Illustrated Handbook to Reigate	R F D Palgrave
Discovering Reigate Priory	A Ward
A History of Reigate Priory	E Sears
Gentlemen of Merstham and Gatton	A B de M. Hunter
Fire over England	T Powell
Royalists, Roundheads and Rogues	B Potter
The Howards of Norfolk	N Grant
The Dukes of Norfolk	J M Robinson
Dissolution of the Monastries	Pitkin Guide
Life in a Monastry	Pitkin Guide
Food and Feast in Tudor England	A Simm
A Chronicle of Folk Customs	B Day
Medieval Holidays and Festivals	M Pelner Cosman
The Yorkist Age	P M Kendal
The Princes in the Tower	A Weir
Henry VIII and his six wives	A Weir
Tudors and Stuarts	R J Unstead
Shakespeare's Kings	J J Norwich
The Earlier Tudors	J D Mackie
The Reign of Elizabeth	J B Black
Surrey, A County History	J Janaway

INDEX

TIME LINE

Year	Reigate and the Howards	National Events
1415	Death of Thomas Fitzalan at the Siege of Harfleur.	English Victory at the the Battle of Agincourt.
1440	Manor of Reigate assigned to the Mowbray Dukes of Norfolk and Earl Marshals of England.	
1450		Loss of France.
1451	Earldom of Surrey and Warenne revived in favour of John Mowbray, son of Duke of Norfolk.	
1455		Wars of Roses begin.
1461	John Howard knighted at Towton.	Yorkists win the throne of England.
1478	Marriage of Anne Mowbray to Richard of York..	

Year	Howard Family Events	National Events
1481	Anne Mowbray dies.	
1483	John Howard made Duke of Norfolk. Visits Reigate to put down Buckingham's rebellion.	Death of Edward IV. Disappearance of the two princes in the Tower. Richard III becomes King.
1485	John Howard killed. His son Thomas Howard, Earl of Surrey, A prisoner in the Tower of London.	Battle of Bosworth. King Richard III killed. Henry Tudor becomes King Henry VII.
1487		Battle of Stoke ends the Wars of the Roses.
1489	Thomas Howard, Earl of Surrey, receives a Royal Pardon.	
1509		Henry VII dies. Henry VIII becomes King of England.
1513	Thomas Howard wins the Battle of Flodden. Promoted to Duke of Norfolk.	War with France and Scotland.

Year	Event	Event
1520		Field of the "Cloth of Gold".
1524	Thomas Howard dies. His son, Thomas, becomes Duke of Norfolk.	
1533		Henry VIII marries Anne Boleyn.
1536	Reigate Priory closed down. Lord Edmund Howard is made Steward of the Priory. Charles Howard born.	Anne Boleyn executed. Henry marries Jane Seymour.
1540		Henry marries Anne of Cleeves following Jane's death.
1541	Reigate Priory granted as a Private home to Lord William Howard.	Henry divorces Anne of Cleeves. Henry marries Catherine Howard.
1542	Lord William Howard arrested.	Catherine Howard beheaded.
1543		Henry marries Katherine Parr
1547	Earl of Surrey executed. Charles Howard begins his education at Reigate Castle.	King Henry VIII dies. Edward VI becomes King.

- **1553** — Edward VI dies. Lady Jane Grey Queen for nine days. Mary I becomes Queen.
  Lord William Howard defends London against Wyatt and comforts Elizabeth in the Tower.
- **1558** — Mary dies. Elizabeth I becomes Queen.
- **1563** — Charles Howard marries Catherine Carey at Bletchingley.
- **1573** — Death of William Howard.
- **1574** — Charles Howard becomes Lord Chamberlain.
- **1585** — Charles Howard becomes Lord Admiral.
- **1588** — Defeat of Spanish Armada.
- **1596** — Raid on Cadiz. Charles Howard is made Earl of Nottingham.
- **1603** — Queen Elizabeth I dies.
  Catherine dies.
- **1604** — James I becomes King.
  Charles Howard re-marries.